within easy reach

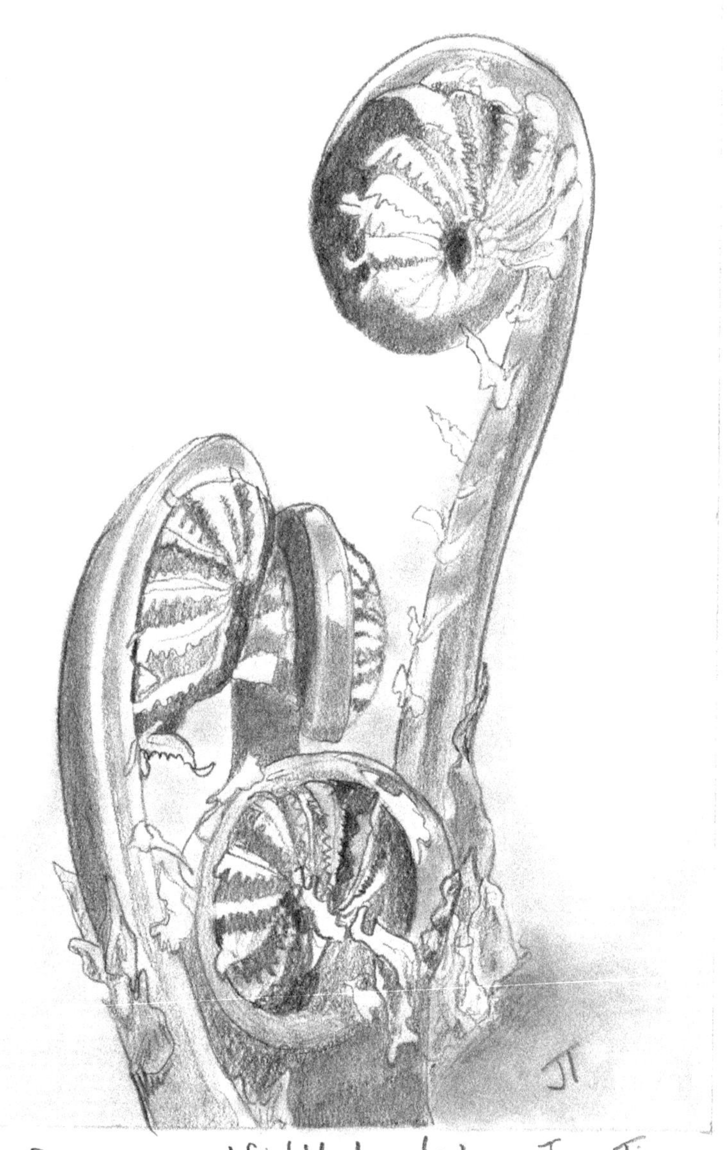

Nov. 5, 2011 'fiddleheads' Jane Tims

within easy reach

poems and drawings by

Jane Spavold Tims

Chapel Street Editions
Woodstock, New Brunswick

Published by
Chapel Street Editions
150 Chapel Street
Woodstock, NB E7M 1H4

www.chapelstreeteditions.com

Library and Archives Canada Cataloguing in Publication

Tims, Jane Spavold, author
Within easy reach / poems and drawings by Jane Spavold Tims.

ISBN 978-1-988299-00-6 (paperback)

I. Title.

PS8639.I568W58 2016 C811'.6 C2016-901454-1

Cover illustration: "brambles" by Jane Spavold Tims

The text is set in Iowan Old Style, a typeface designed by John Downer and released by Bitstream in 1990. It is modeled after earlier revivals of Jenson and Griffo.

Designed by Brendan Helmuth

Disclaimer regarding edible plants:
Although the author and the publisher have made every reasonable effort to ensure the information in this book was correct at press time, the author and publisher do not assume and hereby disclaim any liability to any party for any loss, damage, or disruption caused by errors or omissions, whether such errors or omissions result from negligence, accident, or any other cause.

dedication

to Glen

Contents

Foreword

Jane Tims' *within easy reach* is a veritable farmers' market. Her poem-stalls are piled high with organic fruits, berries, vegetables, and other edible plants, with fish, eggs, honey, and maple syrup, all laden with emotion and brimming with nostalgia and sentiment, but never with sentimentality. Every offering evokes a compelling sense of place, the field, forest, or riverbank from whence it came, places where many of us once were fully present and can be again – seeing, hearing, smelling, touching, tasting, and feeling with both our bodies and our souls.

A remarkable observer of details, Jane quietly "tells it like it was." She writes with the uncomplicated perception and wisdom of a child, bringing her experiences from the past into her present and into ours, making yesterday intimately a part of today. In doing this she enables us not only to reminisce, but also to realise that simple, basic joys are always "within easy reach." Her poem "forty years later" is a perfect example.

Jane's poems suggest even more than they actually say. An undercurrent flows through them all – the sense that every plant, every person, and every experience is connected to the whole, the sense of Gaia. This unstated theme of our connectedness to Creation itself is, perhaps, Jane's greatest offering; she causes us to wonder. We pick a bowl of blueberries or a basket of apples with Jane and ponder All That Is.

Freeman Patterson

Freeman Patterson is a photographer, teacher of visual design, and writer. He is internationally known for his workshops on photography and visual design. He is the author of fourteen books, the latest of which is *Embracing Creation*.

Preface

within easy reach is a collection of poems about gathering local foods. The poems capture the experience of harvesting edible wild plants and foods produced in gardens, orchards, and apiaries. The poems also explore our relationship with nature. They seek to re-establish our connection with nature in the most basic of ways, through growing and gathering our food.

In New Brunswick, many of us eat fiddleheads, blueberries and maple syrup. In coastal areas, some still crave a feed of goosetongue greens. Families enjoy a fall outing in the apple orchard or a June morning picking strawberries. The inspiration for these poems came from an afternoon of picking blackberries with my husband on our property along the Saint John River. We were only a moment or so behind a black bear who was first at the table.

Eating wild and local foods may be part of your family history. In her diaries, written in the 1940s and 1950s, my great-aunt, Anne Ward, living in Tatamagouche, Nova Scotia, mentions picking berries, pickling, fishing, buying local eggs and going to nearby wharves for shellfish. Mom regularly canned vegetables and ate berries, mushrooms, and dandelion greens. Dad grew up on a farm and loved picking berries.

Nevertheless, for lots of people, the grocery store is the place to go to for food, rather than the local farmers' market, the roadside stand, the field or the woods. One purpose of these poems is to encourage the reader to reconnect with nature and use the foods it offers.

The poems celebrate the colours, textures and tastes of gathering local food. Some poems acknowledge the barriers to 'eating local' – the prickles in the blackberry patch and the year-long availability of raspberries from California. Some are about conservation. Other poems are about building relationships and sharing experiences – picking berries, gathering eggs, sitting down for a seasonal meal. Many of the poems are about place – the orchard, the farmers' market, the spring woodland.

Eating local is as simple as visiting a farmers' market and sampling local food in season. If your explorations take you to the field, roadside or woodland remember – identifying plants can be tricky. Never eat any plant if you are not absolutely certain of the identification. Never eat any plant if you have or may have personal sensitivities to it or its components or derivatives. And, never eat any plant unless you have verified its edibility.

Jane Tims
Rusagonis, New Brunswick
2015

Acknowledgements

Some of these poems have appeared elsewhere, in *The Amethyst Review* ("bitter blue"), *Canadian Stories* ("beekeeper", "gathering eggs", "greenhouse, early spring", "small-scale economy"), *CAROUSEL* ("berries in bottles", "cactus berries"), *The Fiddlehead* ("old man's beard"), *Galleon* ("carrot tops", "picking fiddleheads", "where we step"), *Lion's Head Press* ("berries in cellophane"), and *PRISM international* ("beaked hazelnuts"), as well as at www.nichepoetryandprose.wordpress.com.

The manuscript "within easy reach" won Honourable Mention in the 2013 Writing Competition and the poem "rhubarb" won 2nd Place in the 2012 International Quill Quarrel contest.

Many thanks to Gail Taylor who has mentored me over the years and gave thoughtful, detailed observations on several of the poems. I also thank the members of *Wolf Tree Writers* and *Fictional Friends* who provided many helpful comments and suggested revisions. As well, I am grateful to the regular readers of my blog www.nichepoetryandprose.wordpress.com, who read my posts about "growing and gathering", leaving encouraging feedback on posted poems.

I also appreciate the insight of my son, Michael, and other members of my family who listened patiently and offered suggestions. In particular, I want to thank my husband, Glen, who accompanied me on the field trips to find particular plants. He also listened to every poem and steadfastly refused to sample any of my gatherings and concoctions.

I would like to thank Jennie Love for permission to use her photograph in the making of the drawing "fiddleheads". I also thank Shirley Craig for allowing me to use a quote from Philip R. Craig's book *Vineyard Enigma* (the quotation is used with permission of the Estate of Philip R. Craig). Also, thank you to the band Toad the Wet Sprocket for use of lines from the song *Something to Say*.

I am grateful to **artsnb** for the support of a Creation Grant during the writing and preparation of the manuscript.

in a wooden box

"... and I shall need
Two pails..."

Richard Wilbur, *Blackberries for Amelia*

within easy reach

Choke-cherry (*Prunus virginiana* L.)

Choke-cherries flow
into pail, sunlight
into winter, glint
of ripening by fireside
and flame, a taste
of dry wine, cherry-laden
and summer within
easy reach, berries
by the handful, ice-pellets
against the glass [1]

1 Choke-cherry is a large weedy shrub, found along roadways, at the edge of fields and woods, and in barrens and lakeside thickets. The dark red berries occur in drooping clusters. They are very sour but are used to make jelly and wine.

six bottles

I reach
for a cluster
of Choke-cherries
and stop

stretched above me, my grand-mother's hand, dry as a page
from her recipe book, age-spotted, worn at the edges
fingers and ankles swollen, but she is determined –
pick enough berries
for a half-dozen bottles
of burgundy jam

an offering of berries

"… Dott called with a box of berries for me."
Anne Ward, diary entry, July 31, 1957

she stands on the stoop
presents a wooden box
a brimming pint
of berries

I take her hand and we ripple
through the pasture, strew blue
ribbons over bushes, stir
a blueberry jelly sky, dance
with dragonflies

she waits on the stoop
her brow a frown –
for you, she says
a box of berries

JT
Nov. 12, 2011
'five blue berries'
Jane Tims

small-scale economy

my box of berries spilled
on the narrow path
between leaves
of *Kalmia* and wintergreen
hawkweed and cow pies

the cousins, boxes brimming
stood gawking, dismayed
I was certain they were thinking
dumb city girl, spilled her berries
box only half full anyway

but they gathered around me
sympathy in every hand
scooped most of the berries
into the box, added a few
from nearby bushes

seventeen cents he paid me
half the value of a box at full
the cousins had picked a crate or more
remembered the wasted berries, left on the trail
and wept at the loss [2]

---

2 Low Sweet Blueberry (*Vaccinium angustifolium* Aiton) is a woody shrub found on dry, acidic soils in open woodlands, barrens, and waste areas, particularly after burning. Low Sweet Blueberry is also known as Late Sweet Blueberry and Sweet Hurts. *Vaccinium* comes from the Latin *vaccinus* meaning "of cows". The blue berries are eaten raw or in pies and other desserts. They can also be dried or used to make wine.

mended by raspberries

for Mary

drove all the way to Flume Ridge
to pick those berries, large as thimbles

red as blood after we'd pricked
our fingers on needled vines

crossed the covered bridge to nowhere
the through road blocked, the way broken

the covered bridge at our backs
the roar of the flume in our ears

the tipple of honey bees
lightheaded in the berry canes [3]

3 Wild Raspberry (*Rubus strigosus* Michx.) is a prickly bramble found growing in tangled patches in clearings and barrens, and along roadsides and borders of woods. The berries are eaten raw, used to make jam and jelly, or combined with vinegar to make raspberryade.

forty years later

I turn in at the farmhouse
I ring the bell, she

opens the inside door, peers
at me through the screen

she has grey hair, grey eyes
sturdy brown hands

I describe the raspberries
red, plump and seedy

grow just beyond the corner
of the two track road

I explain about the gate
the padlock, the chain

I tell her about Sara
summer vacation

afternoons and berry jam –
she takes the keys from

a hook on the wall, a tub
from the high cupboard

and Sara and I
together again
go picking berries

uncertain strategies

"… and she feeds you tea and oranges
that come all the way from China."

Leonard Cohen, *Suzanne Takes You Down*

berries in cellophane

In the raspberry patch
wary of prickles, we pick
our baskets of berries

Try not to step on the turtle
first inhabitant of the thicket
Deep, we find evidence of bears

berries inhaled by the pawful
and canes pressed into mattresses
studded with thorns

In summers when rain is rare
and berries cling hard and dry
we eat raspberries shipped

from California, wrapped in plastic
boxes to aggravate ears and slash at fingers
Turtles snooze unmolested

Bears lie on their prickly beds
stare at clouds and ponder
grocery lists, compare prices

JT
May 12, 2012 'Serviceberry flowers' Jane Tims

grocery list

Serviceberry (*Amelanchier sanguinea* var. *alnifolia* (Nutt.) P. Landry)

you are the average consumer
you pull a grocery list
from your pocket

cultivated blueberries
jumbo raisins
pears from Oregon

outside the window
a shift in attitude
catches your eye

Serviceberry bushes lean and sway
offer cupfuls of berries – Sugar Pears
flavour of almonds

berries for muffins
magenta jelly
fortified jam

you tear the list into tiny
pieces fall like petals
Amelanchier in June [4]

---

4 Serviceberry is a common shrub, often found on disturbed sites, along roadways and at the edge of fields. Serviceberry is also known as Shadbush, Juneberry, Sugar Pear, and Saskatoon. In late spring, Serviceberry beautifies the landscape with its frail white petals. The fruit of *Amelanchier* is dark purple and berry-like. The fruit is edible and sweet, and can be eaten raw or used to make jam.

the shad are running

after hard rain
and thin wind
between cold front and warm
riverbanks overflow
and for dinner we have fiddleheads
potatoes and shad, served
with last summer's Serviceberry jam

Serviceberry bushes are torn fish nets
holes poked through with fingers
white petals scattered over mossy stones
on the river shore

rooibos in compost

> " ... rooibos tea is made from the leaves of a legume, the redbush..."
> - description on the back of a box of tea

in December
white-tailed deer inspect
the compost heap, nuzzle
snow for carrot tops
tea-bags and apple cores
a fine breakfast, served
under a white cloth

deer uncover delicacies –
ends of green beans, shells of peas
discerning as a hand hovering
over the breakfast buffet, selects
tea from a hardwood box, chooses
a particular muffin, the one with
pineapple and macadamia nuts

in June, we rake the compost
into rows of baby carrots
all summer, we add scraps
to the heap
next winter, deer discover
rooibos under snow
discard bags, strings, labels

deer love all legumes
even imported

north shore smelts

> "… had Charlie, Lena and Madge for tea. I had smelts.
> made biscuits…"
>
> Anne Ward, diary entry, April 29, 1957

1.

A white panel truck parks
in a muddy side-yard
rear doors open. Two
men inside, elbows on knees,

discouraged at sales
ready to quit the day,
to slam the hatch,
search out supper.

They perch on plastic coolers
packed with fish and ice,
fresh with the smells of river,
fish poured in, tails by heads by tails.

2.

I remember smelting
at the mouth of the river
under the metal bridge.
We scooped smelts by the pail

or the dip net,
fish slippery and silver.
Slice their bellies, sever their heads,
scrape out entrails with a fingernail.

Dredge in flour, pan-fry in butter.
The backbone lifts, a skeleton
of slivers, an effigy of fish,
heads buried in the garden.

July 22, 2012 'Indian Cucumber-root' Jane Tims

reasons for the harvest

Indian Cucumber Root (*Medeola virginiana* L.)

subsistence

Hunting and gathering –
an uncertain strategy
Some seasons plentiful, some lean
One rule must be obeyed –
take less than you leave

sustenance

To live local, seek balance
in every acquisition –
a little of this, a little of that

emergency

Left the trail, got topsy-turned
Every tree, a maple
Patch of Cucumber Root – fortunate find
more solace than nutrition

sorcery

Medea sighs between
Fawn-lily and fern
seeks an herbal cure –
a woodland plant
purple berries
two tiers of leaves
a tuber, buried deep

curiosity

The flora describes
the thumb-sized corm
of *Medeola,* crisp edible
flavour of cucumber [5]

5 Indian Cucumber Root is found in rich, acid woods. The common name comes from the cucumber taste of the root, and its traditional use by people of the First Nations. *Medeola* has two whorls of leaves and small white flowers on a slender stem. The berries are dark purple and inedible. The edible, horizontal, white tuber is tasty but should be harvested only rarely, if at all, to conserve the species. The plant, once thought to have medicinal powers, is named after the sorceress Medea.

JT
May 28, 2012
'Bunchberry'
Jane Tims

along the woodland path

Bunchberry (*Cornus canadensis* L.)

follow the trail, tread lightly –
leaf-whorls of Bunchberry are cobblestones
the green-between

ground-creepers
and landing platforms of Bracken
Wild Sarsaparilla

elevated ways for fairy-folk
white flowers shine, guideposts
through the forest

bunches of berries, red-heaped into aprons
pudding for dinner, or winter-fare
gleaned by a gatherer, flavoured by fire

a nibble to cheer a hiker
lost in the woods [6]

---

6 Bunchberry grows in cool woods and barrens, along roadsides and on slopes. It is low-growing and creeps via root-like stems. Bunchberry is also called Crackerberry, Dwarf Cornel, and Pudding-berry. Bunchberry has a short woody stem with a false whorl of six leaves and, below, a smaller pair of leaves. The whorls of leaves are all at the same level in the forest, creating a single "surface" of green. The dazzling white flower of *Cornus canadensis* blooms from May to July and is composed of four petal-like bracts enclosing a central cluster of tiny purplish flowers. The berries of Bunchberry ripen in late summer and are bright scarlet, held in a tight cluster. The berries contain a large seed, but are a sweet trailside nibble. They can also be made into jam or a berry pudding.

JT
May 26, 2012
'Trout Lilies'
Jane Tims

trout lily

(*Erythronium americanum* Ker Gawl.)

On a hike in the hardwood
north of the Dunbar Stream
you discover Trout Lily profusion

Mottled purple leaves overlap
as the scales of adder or dragon
You know these plants as edible

the leaves a salad, or pot-herb
and, deep underground, the corm
flavoured like garlic

You fall to your knees
to dig, to gather, and
hesitate

examine your motives
You, with two granola bars in your knapsack
and a bottle of water from Ontario [7]

7 Trout Lily is an herbaceous, colonial plant, covering slopes in rich, moist hardwoods. Trout Lily is also known as Dog's Tooth Violet, Yellow Adder's-tongue, Fawn-lily, and, in French, *ail doux*. The yellow, lily-like flowers bloom from March to May. The leaves are mottled in maroon and green. The young leaves and bulb-like "corm" are edible but should only be gathered if the plants are abundant, to conserve the species.

July 17, 2012 'Partridge-berry' Jane Tims

twin-berry, two-eyed seeing

Partridge-berry (*Mitchella repens* L.)

1.

leaves opposite
paired along the vine
two world-views
two ways of knowing

2.

he asks me to try
two-eyed seeing [8]

with my eye -
    Mitchella repens L.
    named by a European
    Latin for creeping
    occupies its niche
    in the forest

with his eye –
    little sister
    "holding hands", [9] underground
    she weaves, she whispers
    spirit of his ancestor

---

8 Two-eyed seeing "… refers to learning to see from one eye with the strengths of Indigenous knowledges and ways of knowing, and from the other eye with the strengths of Western knowledges and ways of knowing,… and learning to use both these eyes together, for the benefit of all." Albert Marshall, Elder, Eskasoni First Nation, Nova Scotia, see Cheryl M. Bartlett, "Integrative Science / *Toqwa'tu'kl Kjijitaqnn*: The Story of Our Journey in Bringing Together Indigenous and Western Scientific Knowledge", in Tim Bernard, Leah M. Rosenmeier, and Sharon L. Farrell, *Ta'n Wetapeksi'k: Understanding From Where We Come*, Proceedings of the 2005 Debert Research Workshop, Debert, Nova Scotia, 2011, 182.

9 Chief Charles Labrador, Elder, Acadia First Nation, Nova Scotia, see Murdena Marshall, "*L'nuita'si: Mi'kmaw* Tribal Consciousness", in Tim Bernard, Leah M. Rosenmeier, and Sharon L. Farrell, *Ta'n Wetapeksi'k: Understanding From Where We Come*, Proceedings of the 2005 Debert Research Workshop, Debert, Nova Scotia, 2011, 173.

3.

Twin-berry, Partridge-berry
minijg [10]
Two-eyed Berry gives
form to the hummock
food to the Ruffed Grouse
drapes the stump in new skin
Running Fox between
Mayflower and moss

4.

he asks me to sample
one scarlet berry
seedy, aromatic
quick food along the trail
or a gathering for winter

he asks me to leave
a small offering for the forest

5.

two waxy bells
so near they build
a single berry –
two blossom scars
two eyes [11]

---

10 the Mi'kmaq word for "berry", pronounced *mi-nichk*

11 Partridge-berry is a small evergreen plant of the woodland. It trails, low to the ground, in shady, mossy woods, sometimes covering moist banks and hummocks with its shiny greenery. Partridge-berry is also known as Twinberry, Snakevine, Running Fox and Two-eyed Berry. The word *repens* is from the Latin for "creeping". Partridge-berries are small, ovoid and opposite on a vine-like stem. The flowers are white or pinkish, and bell-shaped. They occur in pairs – the two flowers are closely united at the base, sharing a single calyx. As a result, the bright red berries are two-eyed, each showing two blossom scars. The berries are dry and seedy but edible, with a slightly aromatic flavour. They are a good nibble along the trail or can be used as emergency food. The berries are eaten by Ruffed Grouse and other birds.

storing resilience

Black Spruce weeps if wounded
oozes to heal, embeds
pain in amber, hardened

trails of tears, the eye
rubbed raw, stalactites
in a sorrowful cave.

Emerge from dark, risk
the glow of resin, take
the difficult walk, first steps

in the forest. Consider the woodsman –
carves a box with the point
of his knife, pries gum from the tree

to store for a later chew
pocket of balm and balsam.

May 28, 2012
'Water Dragon'
Jane Tims

desperate harvest

"… they can be satisfied with bark-bread, or cakes made of the roots of water-dragon, which grows wild on the banks of the river…"
Mrs Campbell Overend, 1872

beside the road, the pond
simmers, a kettle
of frog-croak and Leather-leaf
spathes of Water Dragon
hug their lampposts, glow white
entice the desperate

bull-frog song, deepens the shallows
the way voices lower when they
speak of trouble, famine, people
so hungry, harvest so
poor, they wade in mire
grind roots of Wild Calla for flour

needles to tongue, burns to throat
crystals of calcium oxalate, toxic
but worth the risk –
the drying, bruising, leaching, the boil
the painful test to know
if poison has been neutralized

double-edged deliverance
of the *Missen bread* [12]

---

12 Wild Calla (*Calla palustris* L.) is an aquatic plant, found in cold bogs, or along the margins of ponds, lakes and streams. It is also known as Water Dragon, Female Dragons, Frog-cups, and Swamp-Robin. The tiny flowers of Wild Calla grow along a thick spike known as a "spadix". The spadix is enclosed by a leafy bract called the "spathe". The spathe of Wild Calla is bright white, ovoid and abruptly narrow at the tip. The leaves are glossy green and heart-shaped. The various parts of the Wild Calla are poisonous since they contain crystals of calcium oxalate. These cause severe irritation of the mouth and throat if eaten. Nevertheless, Scandinavian people, in times of severe hardship, prepared flour for "Missen bread" from the dried, ground, bruised, leached, and boiled seeds and roots of Wild Calla.

in sumac shade, with lemonade

Staghorn Sumac (*Rhus typhina* L.)

Sumac clones itself,
sculpts light, surfaces
of shade, bark velvet-
flocked. The winter deer
nip lowest buds, try

to control root creep
loss of sun. Rake leaves,
file your nails, weed
the garden. Just for now,

be content, sit in
umbrella shade, sip
sumac lemonade.
Eat a simple meal,
sandwich of butter

and sumac jam, ignore
slice of the minute
hand, the sumac reds
of autumn, feign non-
chalance with the file.

Deer nibble, sumac
shade stays low, but spreads
like jam, infiltrates
hollows
in the bread. [13]

13 Staghorn Sumac is a small tree or shrub found at forest edges and in wastelands. The shrub has an umbrella-like canopy. Staghorn Sumac is often one of the first plants to invade an area after the soil is disturbed. It spreads by a vigorous underground root system and forms colonies with the oldest trees at the centre, causing dense shade to out-compete other plants. The common name Staghorn is derived from the velvet feel of its bark, reminiscent of the texture of deer antlers. The word sumac comes from the words for "red" in Latin (*sumach*) and Arabic (*summāq*) since its leaves and berries turn brilliant red in autumn. The Staghorn Sumac provides food for birds and deer. Staghorn Sumac berries are used to make a lemon-flavored "sumac-ade" or "rhus juice".

the place where you belong

"… show me your home
Not the place where you live
But the place where you belong…"

Toad the Wet Sprocket, *Something to Say*

rhubarb

1.

when I was a child
sour was just a flavour
first activity of the day
tug a stalk of rhubarb
toss the leaf and snap away
the pink transparent sheath
pitch the stringy bits
and nibble, all morning
tart stem and curly peel

2.

rhubarb resists
then surrenders
satisfying
humph
red stem and root
part, concede
the argument

3.

in the abandoned field
rhubarb flowers, white plumes
mark the unpicked patch
garden, cellar and well
left behind, untended

Nov. 25, 2011
'apple tree'
Jane Tims

ripe apples

1.

the tree leans
across the road
drops apples
on the asphalt
creates a shadow of self

2.

thud –
    another
    apple
    fall
I cringe
a dog barks
in the next yard
a wasp rises
from rotting pulp

3.

pressed for cider
strained for jelly
or where they lie, fermented
not an apple wasted

orchard outing

wooden bushel baskets
of laughter, delirious tumble down
the avenue of trees, shadows ripple
among the dapples, Cortlands tied
with scarlet ribbons
burdened
boughs

my son grown tall
on his father's shoulders
stretches to pick the McIntosh
with the reddest shine
small hand
barely able
to grip the apple

apple tree, out of place

> "… small bitter apples
> nobody eats
> even children know better…"
> Al Purdy, *Detail*

before I could spice
applesauce or mull
cider, this woodland
was a green meadow
fenced and dotted

with chicory, grass
and cow pies, cattle
cudding, bumblebees
daisy chains, berries
in sun-drenched spring

but cattle were sold
and saplings over-
topped grass, apple tree
struggled to thrive
under shadow

spruce and fir, bound
by spider thread, layers
of Woodfern arch
Hair Cap mosses
cushion apple

fall, red and ready
to pick but small
and scabby, apple crop
constrained by forest

apple tree
out of place

July 5, 2012
'picking berries'
Jane Tims

land for sale

two acres of waterfront
one of cleared field
one of woods
    Silver Maple and curly fern
    rocky shore

transparent water, wobbling waves
an island over there
conservation land
    no buildings to interrupt
    the view

we make plans –
the house here
the driveway, and a gate
    a garden
    and a path
    through the maples
    to the shore
    and a dock

two good-natured chairs
one beside the other
bonfires in July
skating in January
price within reason
    promising neighbours

and the clincher?
the deal maker?
the heart breaker?
    a crooked bush
    with five fat blueberries
    ready to pick

greed

"... she puts jellybeans in her gravy..."
(euphemism for lumpy gravy, from an old family story)

jealous of the shore land's pretty
shaped and rounded stones
the ocean mutters
claws them back
clatters its dinner forks
over biscuits, salt greens and gravy
hoards pebbles
jellybeans by the handful

June 14, 2012 'Sea-Blite, Oak Bay' Jane Tims

persuasion

Sea-blite (*Suaeda maritima* (L.) Dumort.)

Sea-blite fingers
poke the salt air
salute the salt sea
crave attention –

pick me! pick me!!

Sea-blite fingers
point at the pot
propose, diplomatically, *please add*
a little more salt [14]

14 Sea-blite is a low-growing plant, often forming mats on the coastal shore. The plant can also be found at inland locations, near salt springs. Sea-blite has thick, linear leaves. These are very salty, and can be used as a pot-herb, an ingredient in salads, or a source of salt in soup or stew.

sunday dinner at maces bay

Seaside Plantain (*Plantago juncoides* Lam.)

dig right in
says your father
and nudges the pitcher of water
in my direction

I study the *goosetongue greens* –
like spaghetti between
spuds and chicken
eels diving for
the bottom of the plate

two things not in their favour –
they're green
they look a little like
the tongues of geese

I watch your dad –
he adds a dollop of butter
he weaves his fork to catch a little of each –
potato, greens and chicken
he chews with his eyes closed
reaches for his glass

I sigh
and taste –
salt air and butter cream
crisp, the perfect crush
mouth-feel amazing
please pass the water [15]

15 Seaside Plantain, also known as Goosetongue, is a coastal plant, growing in a thick carpet on the shore. The succulent, linear leaves of Seaside Plantain occur in a basal rosette and are grey-green in color. Goosetongue greens are salty, a local delicacy, eaten as a salad or pickle, or cooked like green beans and served with butter.

June 14, 2012 'Orach, Oak Bay' Jane Tims

where the orach grows

1.

At the ankle-wet edge of the waves
breathe salt-fresh air, thick
with fishing weirs, sea foam and fog
Study the crisp edge, the tolerance
of islands, rocks and wind-formed trees
Choose the place to stand –
twelve hours to know if you have stepped
too far, at least to wet your thighs and wrists
at most to comprehend where ocean can drown you
carry you away

2.

At low tide, who can know what marker to choose?
Somewhere, unforgiving, up-shore of the flats
where clams, best filters of detritus, spurt their stories
Perhaps the first, second or third band of bladderwrack
or the place where hydrophylics flourish –
clumps of Goosetongue, mats of Sea-blite
forks of Samphire, salt for the stew, delicacies from the strand
Or where the Orach grows, at the landward threshold
of salt air, salt spray but where salted waters
rarely stray [16]

---

16 Orach (various species of *Atriplex*) is a coastal plant with triangular leaves, found growing in sand or between rocks. Orach can be used as a nibble, a salad green or a cooked vegetable.

Samphire (*Salicornia europaea* L.) is a pale green plant growing in salt marshes and tidal flats. It has a succulent, jointed stem without apparent leaves or flowers. The salty plants are used as a salad green or potherb, and can be pickled.

where we step

1.

my brother and I explore
the old home place, overgrown
the house fallen into the cellar
a sock tossed into a dresser drawer

2.

barefoot not an option
even shod, we are careful
of our feet–nails, glass
bricks from the chimney
unease creeps beneath the grass
we watch for the water well, covered
but with rotted boards

3.

hard not to love where we step –
    mint enfolds our ankles
    rose and rosemary our minds
    chives lace our sneakers
    flowers from purple papers
    lavender leans on walls

4.

silvered, graceful and wise
the sage surveys our ruin
and thyme is bruised
everywhere we step

pick faster

"We pick them in the hot
slow-motion of midmorning."

Robert Hass, *Picking Blackberries with a
Friend Who Has Been Reading Jacques Lacan*

bitter blue

for Mom

of all the silvery summer days we spent   none so warm   sun on granite boulders   round blue berry field   miles across hazy miles   away from hearing anything but bees

and berries
plopping in the pail

beside you   I draped my lazy bones on bushes   crushed berries and thick red leaves over moss   dark animal trails nudged between rocks   berries baking brown   musk rising to meet blue heat

or the still fleet scent
of a waxy berry bell

melting in my mouth   crammed with fruit   sometimes pulled from laden stems   more often scooped from your pail   full ripe blue pulp and the bitter shock of a hard green berry never ripe

or a shield bug
with frantic legs
and an edge to her shell

pick faster

for Dad

blue ripens as morning, deft fingers
noisy pails, hail on metal gutters
this bush spent, unsatisfactory
berries over there fatter
bluer

I am certain I see, beside mine
my father's hands, callused
and quick

berries roll between
thumb and fingers

I try to meet
his expectation

pick faster

beaked hazelnuts

(*Corylus cornuta* Marshall)

"… these fallen hazel-nuts,
stripped late of their green sheaths…
I bring you as offering."
Hilda Dolittle, *Orchard*

paired hazelnuts hang
husks curve
translucent, lime
they ripen
this year, they are mine

uptight red squirrels agitate, on guard, we watch
the hazelnuts ripen, slow as cobwebs falling, nut pies
browning through the glass of the oven door
green berries losing yellow, making blue
dust motes in a crook of light
float, small hooked hairs
shine
two more days

hesitate
and red squirrels
bury their hazelnuts [17]

---

17 The Beaked Hazelnut is a wiry shrub found in mixed woods. The edible nut is contained in a bristly, beaked husk.

picking choke-cherries by a dusty road

Choke-cherry (*Prunus virginiana* L.)

1.

first rinse
road dust washed
from purple gloss

2.

strip the
branches
quicken
fill the pails
pause to wave
as cars honk
flog road dust
follow the river

the unpaved
track to the village
ascends, dust dances
settles on white flowers
purple drupes

burdened bushes
lean across the ditch
painless pulling into pail
berries flow, deciduous
as water or Choke-cherry wine

3.

rinse away the dust of summer
unripe berries clog the drain
the best float
purple
pungent
pure

contrails

I observe my hands manoeuvre
between branches, bowl half full and I
can't recall the picking, amber
light and can't remember the last
ten minutes of driving. Hands toss
a few berries into the bowl
and I wonder if the cable

bill was paid, or if I thanked Em
sincerely for her meatloaf. Some-
one across the field *halloos,* points
to zenith, the intersection
of three vapour trails. Hands miss their
rhythm, and a green berry fails
detection, burrows into the

bowl, ahead of fumbling fingers.
I remember turning eight, yet
to understand there was a skill
to picking berries. Took the time
to match them like pearls, proud when
the bottom of the pail vanished
under the first layer of bearings.

thirsty wind

Saskatoon (*Amelanchier alnifolia* (Nutt.) Nutt. ex M. Roem.)

along the shelterbelt
Saskatoons, pendulant
tease the hot dry wind tries

to lift berry branches
from my fingers grasp
the limb, steady the picking

enough for a Saskatoon
berry pie cools on the Formica
table, chromed legs and linoleum

inward drift of the curtain
carries the thirst of the wind
goal to lap each molecule of steam

as it scrolls from the pie, to seek
every seam and seep, every sequestration
of prairie water

berries in bottles

Cloudberry (*Rubus chamaemorus* L.)

they stand at the edge of the road
children, arms stretched outward
rigid, hair *all mops and brooms*, she says
quart jars filled with amber berries
and water

grew over there, out on the berry ground
they say, sweeping arms
take in all of the boggy barren
along the Avalon Peninsula road

what are they called?
baie qu'appelle? she asks
that's right, *bakeapples*
baygabbles, they say
for wine and for jam
and syrup for ice cream

she says, *shouldn't they be red?*
you don't eat the red ones, they're green
taste like apricots
and honey, they say
smell like feet

they sag, so weary, these entrepreneurial urchins
a single berry to a stem
whole bottle well worth a ten [18]

---

18 Cloudberry is a dwarf herbaceous bramble, found in peat bogs, barrens and meadows. Cloudberries are also known as Bakeapples or Bake-apple-berries. The plants are low-growing and have no prickles. The yellow or peach-colored berries ripen in July and August. The berries are eaten raw or used to make wine, jelly or jam.

manoeuvring in thorns

> "A blackberry alley, going down in hooks, and a sea
> Somewhere at the end of it, heaving..."
>
> Sylvia Plath, *Blackberrying*

family reunion

for four members of the bedstraw "family":
Rough Bedstraw (*Galium asprellum* Michx.)
Wild Madder (*Rubia peregrina* L.)
Cleavers (*Galium aparine* L.)
Sweet-scented Bedstraw (*Galium triflorum* Michx.)

I know about difference –
just look at me and my cousins
I am a liar, tell stories
they listen, add detail to narrative, some laugh
some bring covered casseroles
to the picnic

my tales are sticky, tangled
as Rough Bedstraw
under tables in the orchard
as red as tablecloths
dyed from the root
of Wild Madder

I hide my hands behind my back
crossed fingers, crossed ankles
the criss-crossed legs
of the wooden chairs
cousins line up
for Aunt Edith's pies

potato salad with shoots of Cleavers, chopped
(prepared by a cousin who wears Earth Shoes, went back to nature)
they won't be trying Emily's meatloaf
(food poisoning last summer)
I fill a mug with Earth Cousin's substitute coffee
made from the nutlets of Cleavers, dried and roasted and ground

I settle, under a tree in the orchard
in Sweet-scented Bedstraw
I test the mattress, flower-freckled and fragrant
I should sit at the table, hug Emily, sample her meatloaf
tell a story about the perils of drinking
coffee in bed [19]

19 Rough Bedstraw is a common sprawling weed with weak stems. It reclines on other vegetation, forming a tangle across low pastures, brooksides and ditches. The tangle looks springy and comfortable, but the stem feels rough and sticky when rubbed backwards, due to the plant's rasping, hooked prickles.

The bedstraw family includes many useful species. Wild Madder is used to make a red dye and Cleavers is a coffee substitute. People have used Rough Bedstraw and Sweet-scented Bedstraw to stuff mattresses because the smell of the dried plants repels fleas.

berry picking

fingers stain indigo
berry juice as blood
withdrawn by eager thorns

berry picking sticks to me, burrs
and brambles, hooks and eyes, inseparable
as my hands and picking berries

and if I struggle to be free
berries ripen, shake
loose, fall
to ground

spring break-up

Marsh Blue Violet (*Viola cucullata* Aiton)

After snow melts, ice
thaws and woods are wet
we walk along the brook, hooded
hands in pockets

To shock him I rip a stalk
and a leaf from the muck where
purple violets swarm, I show him
the color, the shape – an envious heart
I gnaw the leaf, swallow it
serrated edges
and all

Later, I pick a bunch of leaves
crush them, steep them, sip the tea
decorate a cake with violets
celebrate loss [20]

---

20 The Marsh Blue Violet, also known as the Purple Violet, the Hooded Blue Violet, and the Long-stemmed Marsh Violet, is a low-growing perennial preferring wetlands or low wet areas in mixed or coniferous woods. The Latin species name means "hooded" from the inrolled young leaves. The leaves are often heart-shaped, with rounded teeth. The Marsh Blue Violet blooms in May. The leaves can be eaten raw or cooked, used as a thickener in soup, or to make tea. The flowers can be added to a salad or used for edible decoration.

risk

Hawthorn (*Crataegus spp.*)

each fall, the Hawthorn bleeds
with berries, impales
  with thorns

berries are difficult to gather
easier to flood, with red
  imagination

to strip the bush of every drop
Cretaegus draws
  so choose –

ignore the feast, or risk
a bleed to pick a berry
  collude with birds

see how waxwings hover
twig to twig, manoeuvre
  in the thorns

haws, of course, not wasted –
what red the thrushes leave
  will rot

nourish another season [21]

---

21 The Hawthorn is a woody shrub or bush with sharp thorns, growing in thickets and along rivers, lakes and coastal areas. Hawthorn is also called Red Haw. The red, fleshy fruit is used to make tea, jelly or jam.

wolf river apple blossoms

Apple blossoms pop
like corn, and bees explore
for precursors of wax

and honey, I have
a premonition
of apple, stretch

but skyward branches
flaunt their produce
a fingertip away

We had big
plans for this tree
grafts and pruning

a low umbrella
every fruit in easy grasp
The payoffs for neglect –

apples out of reach
fragile wood
apple fire

Bumble bees
stubborn, stumble
blossom

to blossom, investigate
low branches where
the apple ladder takes a break

rotted but not resolved

cactus berries

> "... Biting back fear is one price of parenthood."
> Philip R. Craig, *Vineyard Enigma*

1.

when we were eight, we played
on the prairie, lured by the melon-pink
of mallow, the velvet of its leaves

we ran with the tumbleweed
dodged the rattle
of grasshoppers
tested the long thorns of cactus
greed and respect separated
by the seedy burst of cactus berries

we played the width of the flat
to the cliffs, the edge-work of the river
our sleeves porcupined with spear-grass

2.

my dad watched the two
specks on the prairie
encounters with rattlesnake
topmost on his mind

3.

when I was six
I gave my mother a gift –
a jar of scorpions
glossy, transparent
fresh-picked from the prairie

high school dance 1970

you step outside, hang out
with the smoke-drowsy

as though the beekeeper
shuffles among the honeycombs, calms
the workers with a smouldering rag
and unalarming ways

inside, the gymnasium floor, waxed and slippery
streamers, a ceiling-hung hive
of mirrors, hexagonal reflections
climb the walls

the boy you can't ignore
hangs out in a swarm
with the other drones
a queen bee basks among them

other bees with crinolines
and gossamer wings
circle you, looking for an argument
unprovoked sting

the boy you danced with last month
sits, six-legged on a table in the hall
high as a bee's-nest
when the weatherman predicts

more snow than usual
these dances can make you
cry, honeyed words and nonchalance always
the best strategy

later, red eyes and injured eardrums
propel you through the double-doors
beat quieted to a hum
not quite silence

you head for the parking lot
where your parents wait –
next morning, tears, a headache
honey and toast for breakfast

May 20, 2012
'Bluebead Lily'
Jane Tims
JT

poisonous

White Baneberry
and Bluebead Lily, sly
berries peek, vivid
between leaves, part
a path in the under-
story, dolls wink, use
fern shadow to blink
guile disguised as gift
a bead of metal
lacquered
alien
blue

glossed in the margins
of the Guidebook
with crossbones and skull [22]

---

22 White Baneberry (*Actaea pachypoda* Elliott) is also called Doll's Eyes because the poisonous berry is white with a dark spot and resembles an eyeball. The toxic berry of Bluebead Lily (*Clintonia borealis* (Aiton) Raf.) is a metallic, unnatural blue. Both plants are found in wooded areas.

charming a bee

"… splurge well
in the silent, startled, icy, black language
of blackberry-eating in late September."

Galway Kinnell, *Blackberry Eating*

portrait of the beekeeper

levers of the bellows meet, expel
a wisp of white from the smoker
so hard to paint – his eyes behind
the mesh, his hands anonymous

in gloves, fog on the meadow, bird call
smothered beneath the hum of bees
a worker lights on his glove
the brush of his hand disturbs less

than a shimmer of air, a single
hair from the sable, he eases
a frame from the hive, examines
the comb in perfect light, a bee

lands on my wrist and I do not breathe
unwilling to part with steady
stroke or his profile, the bee lifts
and leaves, the beekeeper fits frame

to hive, an artist, sliding a wet
canvas into its box, ready
for travel, the final painting
hesitates on the gallery

wall, subject matter – dandelion
seed released, stems of Golden Glow
lean against the hive, fog on the meadow
a bee in the dance

beekeeper

1.

bees smoke-drowsy   rag smoulders   swung slowly   protected thick
in net and cotton   wicking folds   into beeswax   candle flame
pours golden   through panes   in the honeycomb
streamers   sweet circles   sink into bread

hollows of air
yeast-filled
and honey

2.

the bee stings

but the beekeeper never flinches
flicks it from his fingers

spit and mud
for a poultice

how to collect honey

Honeysuckle and amber
coil from the spoon
tangle light
For this

you charm a bee
to crawl, hexagonal
on human skin
unalarmed

Adrenalin fear
hidden by the scent
of cherry blossom
and pear

lessons for young mothers

in the summer field
by the split rail fence
the vireo never grows weary
of asking its question

predictable as a child's
are we there yet?
are we there yet?

Alsike and *Lonicera*
flavour the sugar wind
clover-honey and cinnamon
on buttered toast

hold your breath, wait
for the waxwing to reveal
its hiding place

check your list of errands –
strings to gather, mosquitoes
to pluck from the sky, diapers to buy
air to inhale, one lungful at a time

answer the question
follow the compass
mingle exotic with sweet

break from the cover of pine
wings to open air

maple syrup song

cold night
warm day
cold night

sap plucks stainless steel
different rhythm, every tap
quick or dead slow
in sync
with the downy woodpecker
or the bird with the round warble in its throat

JT
May 12, 2012
'picking fiddleheads'
Jane Tims

picking fiddleheads

under your feet, the wetland
a sponge, and last year's ferns
cut-work brown paper laid
across fallen branches

the woods are over-bright
no leaves to shadow
fiddleheads held proud
on lime-green stems

this, you learn quickly
is a labour of reaching and aching backs
next clump and coil
always a finger-tip away

boots shuffle in dry leaves
a twig breaks
you snap a fiddlehead from its stem –
it gives up so easily

you learn efficiency
gather three in one hand
release them to the pail, the other hand
already picking [23]

23 The Ostrich Fern (*Matteuccia Struthiopteris* (L.) Tod.) grows in wet areas along riverways and wetlands. Its leaves first emerge in spring as edible green fiddleheads.

clear waters

I see the salmon
land-locked
between the leaves
of tree shadows

tired of his dawdles
I reel in the line
he follows the lure, across the cove
to the rod's reflection

he takes the hook
eagerly
almost leaps
into my arms

whispers another
fish story
sleek and slippery
too slick to hold

in an altered direction

> "... you will remember nothing
> of your old life..."
>
> Lisel Mueller, *Picking Raspberries*

greenhouse, early spring

dead plantings rustle
skeletons brittle
pods and packets rattle
whisper me to the greenhouse

weak sunshine warms the glass
my prints a path on late snow
melt water sinks into grass
soaks into clay

bits of crockery
wooden handles
leaf mould and sand
soil pressed into pots

the gardener
awakened from winter
rooted in moss and clay

connecting the dots

"... Not until we are lost do we begin to find ourselves..."
Henry David Thoreau, *Walden*

I pick berries all afternoon
bush to bush, clearing to clearing

no thought of keeping the truck
in sight, no problem really –
the stream and the highway
perpendicular to one another
down slope to the stream

but, to be lost, so late in the day –
a night alone in the woods
no thrill
everyone
worried

I retrace my picking, hard to tell
the difference between
my lazy sprawl
and the wallows of a bear
picked his berries yesterday

I connect the dots, berryless bush
to berryless bush, the sun angling down

I find a glade where the bushes show
no signs of picking, where I

began and, over there, my extra
bowl, forgotten in the joy of finding
plentiful berries

I choose a likely heading for the truck
keep my shadow secure to my right

ten minutes, no truck
I panic
frantic
in every direction
heart thuds, I collapse
in gulps, inhale
the forest, stoic trees
and ancient
game trails
slow my
breathing

I think, *at least*
I have food, I eat a berry

I keep my shadow, secure to my left
walk back to the unpicked patch
adjust my fading shadow
walk out
in an altered direction

the blue of the truck echoes the blue of my berries
good amount for an afternoon of picking

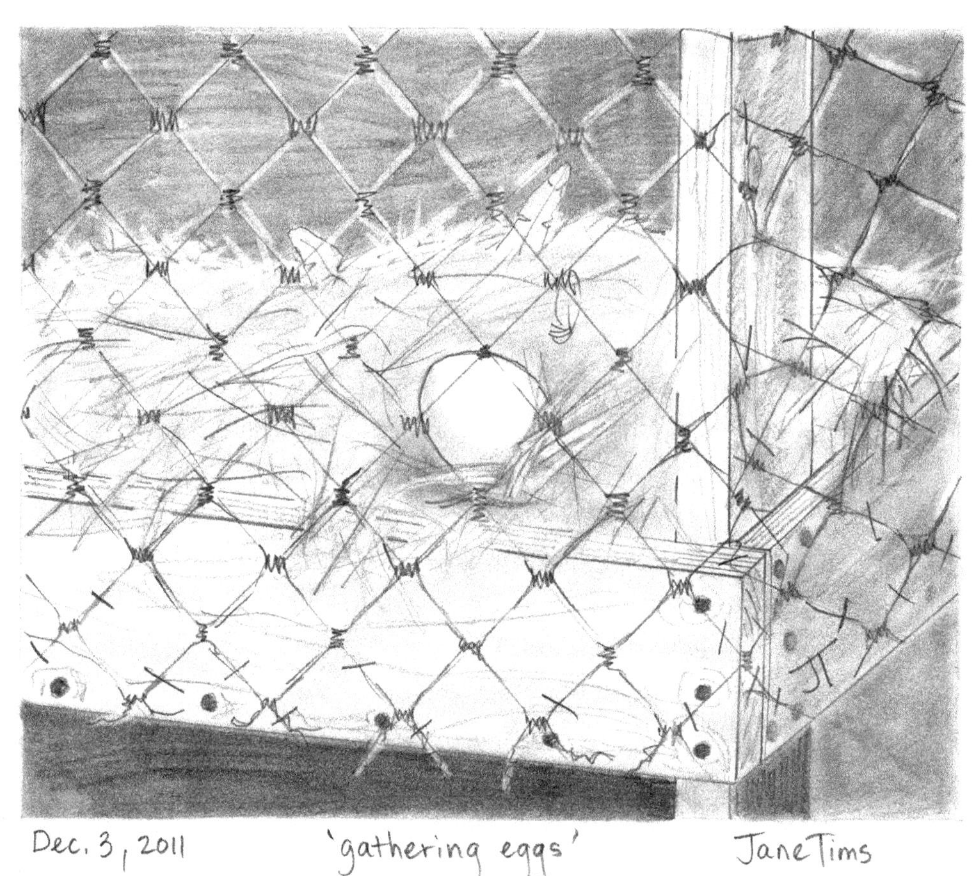
Dec. 3, 2011
'gathering eggs'
Jane Tims

gathering eggs

first breath after rooster presses
crowbar under sun catches
dew in three-angled strawberry leaves
and light pings sapphire
red amber emerald
to opening eyes
see my dog Dandy waiting
black and white counterpoint to rainbow

Dandy greets me taunts
the chickens scratching
along random lines we trek
to the barn together push
the man-door open the pen-door
to the layers within where
Diane has promised

a gather of eggs, shows me how
to shoo the hen, part
the straw, roll the egg
into my hand, build the stack
in the basket, set each
in a three-angled cradle

Dandy watches
the rooster, red comb
and wattles, amber neck
iridescent tail, ignores
white eggs, white chickens

carrot tops

ten AM at the farmers' market
bunches of carrots catch your eye
thick tapered roots
topped with green fern

nearest to a garden you've strayed
in a while, the narrow counter elongates
to a field, neat rows
of froth, carrots and parsley, well-weeded

you reach for a bunch
it lifts from the earth, a shower
of loose soil, leaves
a neat hole in the ground

you turn the carrots, not a trace
of mud, just deep wet orange, spray
of wash water still drips
from tap root and thread

orange the color of pumpkins or the Japanese lanterns
growing at the side of your mother's house
the plastic fruit in the bowl
on the counter in your kitchen

the vendor nudges you with the price
asks if you want the tops
severs the green feathers
tosses them into a cardboard box

beheaded carrots are tucked
into a paper bag
you feel she has
the best of the bargain

you could have begun a compost bin
in the corner of the apartment
walked away with carrot tops
peaking over the edge of the bag

March 18, 2012 'blackberries' Jane Tims

berries in brambles

"... summer's blood was in it..."
Seamus Heaney, *Blackberry-picking*

1.

on the mowed road
above the lake
we are astonished
blackberries
    precocious
    sinister
    delicious

2.

for three Saturdays
we pick berries

first, unprepared
we heap them
into hats
eat handfuls
pulp, seeds and cordial pressed
between palate and tongue

the next
we stay all morning
reach deep into the bushes
thorns impale the easy pull
of berries into pail

all week we concoct
    blackberry jam
    blackberry buckle
    blackberry muffins
set blackberry brandy to steep

the last day
we are uneasy
    (indigo bear droppings
    still steaming)
the picking hard
berries and foreheads
sun-shrivelled
bloody scratches on arms

3.

blackberry
brambles
grapple my coat

more than a firm tug needed
to struggle free [24]

---

24 Blackberries (various species of *Rubus*) are brambles growing in barrens and waste areas, in meadows and along roadsides. Plants range from tall and arching to low-growing. Some have numerous prickles and bristles, and some are barely prickly. The black fruit are raspberry-like, eaten raw, or used to make jam, jelly and beverages.

berry field, grown over

We follow the track,
sniff the air,
strain to see the lake
I frown at the thicket,
the girth of the pines

You sit on a rock –
wrong path, again.
does it even exist?
this 'perfect patch' of berries?

I search for the opening,
the bushes, blue-black with berries
I see only trees,
alder, hardhack, hawkweed

The clearing must hide
just over there,
but pine trees whisper,
unfamiliar

We trudge to the car,
pails empty,
not quite the way we came

Feb. 4, 2012 'wild strawberries' Jane Tims

old man's beard

(*Usnea subfloridana* Stirt.)

you and I
years ago
forced our ways
bent through the thicket
of lichen and spruce

Usnea
caught in your beard
and we laughed
absurd!
us with stooped backs
and grey hair?

found a game trail
a strawberry marsh
wild berries
crushed into sedge
stained shirts
lips
and fingers

strawberries
dusted with sugar
washed down with cold tea
warmed by rum

today
an old woman
    alone
lost her way in the spruce
found beard
    caught in the branches
and cried [25]

25 *Usnea* is a lichen often found growing on old and stressed trees in coniferous woods. The common name, Old Man's Beard, refers to the matted, stringy appearance of the lichen, hanging in clumps from tree branches. Lichens are made up of two species, an alga and a fungus, living together symbiotically.

apple ladder

the ladder leans against the tree, stretches
its length through the shadow
one leg uncertain
where it meets
the damp

the orchard ages
also, broken
branches, tattered
leaves, ragged
bark

wood of ladder, kin
to wood of tree, holds
quiet, strong
adds nothing
to their worries

when you are part of an orchard
you must occupy each
inch of space, devote
your life to apples, honour
every ounce of sap

the reward of solidarity –
    dry apple wood
    compact, efficient
    consistent burn
    rarely a spark

steady, the way the ladder
    served, sturdy
    when called, never
    a crack, devoted
    to the highest apple

a story you know
    very well, ending
    certain
    no foreshadow
    no surprise

Sources for the Epigraphs

Cohen, Leonard. "Suzanne Takes You Down." *Parasites of Heaven*. Toronto: McClelland and Stewart, 1967.

Craig, Philip R. *Vineyard Enigma*. New York: Avon Books, 2002.

Dinning, Dean, Randy Guss, Todd Nichols and Glen Phillips. "Something to Say." *Fear* (Toad the Wet Sprocket). Sony, 1991.

Dolittle, Hilda. "Orchard." *Sea Garden*. London: Constable and Company Ltd., 1916.

Hass, Robert. "Picking Blackberries with a Friend Who Has Been Reading Jacques Lacan." *Praise*. New York: Ecco Press, 1999.

Heaney, Seamus. "Blackberry-picking." *Death of a Naturalist*. London: Faber and Faber, 1966.

Kinnell, Galway. "Blackberry Eating." *Mortal Acts, Mortal Words*. New York: Mariner Books, 1980.

Mueller, Lisel. "Picking Raspberries." *The Need to Hold Still*. Baton Rouge: Louisiana State University Press, 1980.

Overend, Mrs Campbell. *The Besieged City and the Heroes of Sweden*. Edinburgh: William Oliphant and Co.,1892.

Plath, Sylvia. "Blackberrying." *Collected Poems*. London: Faber and Faber, 1981.

Purdy, Al. "Detail." *Wild Grape Wine*. Toronto: McClelland and Stewart, 1968.

Thoreau, Henry David. *Walden*. Boston: Ticknor and Fields, 1854.

Wilbur, Richard. "Blackberries for Amelia." *Mayflies*. London: Waywiser Press, 2004.

List of Illustrations

"**apple tree**" (page 38) drawn from memory, of an old apple tree in my grandfather's orchard; spent many happy hours reading on that convenient horizontal branch

"**picking berries**" (page 42) from a photo of my brother and sister-in-law, picking berries during a drive to Peggy's Cove in Nova Scotia

"**Sea-blite, Oak Bay**" (page 46) a small specimen, still getting established in early spring; drawn after a drive to the shore at Oak Bay in New Brunswick

"**Orach, Oak Bay**" (page 50) drawn after our trip to Oak Bay; this plant was growing between stones at the top of the shore; leaves were pale purple, shaped like arrow-heads

"**Bluebead Lily**" (page 76) from a photo of the single Bluebead Lily plant growing along our fence in the Grey Woods; berries are an alien shade of blue

"**picking fiddleheads**" (page 86) drawn from a photo of two women picking fiddleheads on the Grand Lake Meadows, along the Saint John River, in spring

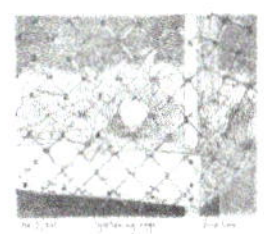

"**gathering eggs**" (page 94) drawn from memory of gathering eggs at my grandfather's farm when I was a child

"**blackberries**" (page 98) from a photo, the same used as subject matter for the cover painting; discovering these berries along the hill at our lake property provided the inspiration for this book and the poem "berries in brambles"

"**wild strawberries**" (page 102) from a photo of the wild strawberries growing in the field at our lake property

About the Author

Jane Spavold Tims is a botanist, historian, artist and writer. She was born and raised in southern Alberta and now lives in rural New Brunswick. She obtained her B.Sc. and M.Sc. in biology at Dalhousie University in Halifax and later returned to university to obtain a B.A. in anthropology and history at the University of New Brunswick in Fredericton. During her career she worked in environmental protection, in the fields of air quality, watershed management, and community planning.

Jane writes poetry and fiction and presents her writing, painting and drawings of plants, birds and landscape at www.janetims.com. Her main interests include identifying plants, collecting wild foods, making natural plant dyes and exploring New Brunswick's covered bridges. She is a member of the Writers' Federation of New Brunswick and an early version of the manuscript for "within easy reach" won Honourable Mention in the 2013 WFNB Writing Competition.

Jane believes in eating local foods. She makes maple syrup from her own trees and loves picking apples, berries, and wild herbs and greens.

Photo by J.D.R. Beaudoin

www.ingramcontent.com/pod-product-compliance
Ingram Content Group UK Ltd.
Pitfield, Milton Keynes, MK11 3LW, UK
UKHW062003290726
14090UKWH00022B/1371

9 781988 299006